Speeding along
the Grand Prix Raceway.

Getting wet inside Splash Mountain.

Riding up and down and around
on Cinderella's Golden Carousel.

Steer clear of the skeleton pirate!

Captain Hook
from Peter Pan's Flight.

The limestone cave
on Tom Sawyer Island.

The Sword in the Stone
in front of Cinderella's Golden Carousel.

20,000 Leagues Under the Sea.

A squid attack!

Bonnie and Kate
outside Splash Mountain.

Lulu and Minnie Moo
are thirsty for some milk.

Awwright—Splash Mountain!

Cinderella is ready for the ball
—and so is Lulu.

Uncle Scrooge with his favorite thing
—money!

MEET ME IN THE MAGIC KINGDOM

KATHY JAKOBSEN

Disney PRESS

NEW YORK

SAY "CHEESE!"

With love to . . .
Becky, Martin, Alana, and Bonnie

FIRST EDITION
1 3 5 7 9 10 8 6 4 2

Library of Congress Catalog Card Number: 94-74961
ISBN: 0-7868-3038-7

The artwork for each picture is prepared using oil paint on canvas.

The big day had finally arrived. Today Kate and her family were going on vacation. She couldn't wait to see her cousin Bonnie. Every summer the two families planned a vacation together in a new place. Kate's mom called it a family tradition. This year they had decided to meet at the *Magic Kingdom* in Florida.

Kate and her brother, Mike, helped Dad and Mom load the van. Mom laughed when Dad complained about bringing too much. "That's part of the family tradition, too," she told Kate.

They were finally on their way! From the highway, Kate saw the jagged skyline of Manhattan in the distance. Now she knew why they called the tall buildings skyscrapers. They seemed to reach up and scrape the sky!

A few hours later Kate's dad pointed to a domed building in the distance. "There's Washington, D.C.," he announced. "The nation's capital!" They toured the Capitol, where the country's laws are made; the Smithsonian

Institution; the Washington Monument; and the Lincoln and Jefferson Memorials. They even visited the White House, where the president and the first family live. Kate's dad took lots of pictures.

Bonnie's family lived in Minnesota, so Uncle Lee and Aunt Karen decided to fly to Florida. It was more than 1,500 miles away. The pilot announced that they would fly over seven states! It would have taken Bonnie and her family about three days to drive, but it took only four hours for them to fly.

From so high up, it was hard to tell one state from another. The land seemed to stretch out in every direction as far as the eye could see. Bonnie thought the farms of Iowa looked like one of her grandmother's giant patch-work quilts.

"Almost there!" announced Kate's dad. Kate and Mike cheered. The drive had been fun, but Kate was anxious to meet up with her cousins in Orlando. That's when the *real* fun would begin.

"Look who's here!" said Kate's dad. Everyone laughed and hugged. That night at the hotel, Kate and Bonnie talked excitedly about all the neat things they would do tomorrow. They couldn't wait!

"There it is!" shouted Kate the next morning. It was early, but Main Street was already crowded with families strolling in and out of the many shops. A horse trotted by pulling a trolley, and the conductor rang a big brass bell. Dad said it reminded him of a small town at the turn of the century.

"Did you take a trolley to work, too?" Mike asked.

"I'm not that old!" Dad laughed.

"Look!" Bonnie shouted. Up ahead the gleaming spires of Cinderella's Castle touched the sky.

The first thing Mike and Rich wanted to do was climb the Swiss Family Treehouse. It had just about everything a real house had, including three levels, wood furniture, lamps, beds with quilts, candles stuck in seashells, even running water.

Uncle Lee suggested they go on a jungle cruise next. Their boat chug-chugged downriver through a jungle in Southeast Asia, the Nile Valley, the African veldt, and the Amazon rainforest. Some elephants onshore were taking a bath. "They splash around more than Lulu!" joked Bonnie.

"Aarrghh!" growled a pirate captain from atop his buried treasure. It was just like being on a pirate raid on a Caribbean island town in the 1800s. Pirates were everywhere. There was even a parrot dressed in a pirate costume!

It was easy to understand how Splash Mountain got its name. No one stayed dry as the log plunged down the giant waterfall with a huge *SPLASH!* Kate and Bonnie sat in front—and got soaked!

At the entrance to the Haunted Mansion, Kate read the funny inscriptions on the tombstones in the graveyard. She worried if it might be a little scary inside, but Bonnie said, "It's fun to be scared."

Bonnie was right. The ghosts and goblins danced and sang and flew through the air. It was a huge ghost party. One of them even sat on Kate's lap. "Hey, Kate," said Bonnie, "I think that ghost wants a ride!"

After a break for lunch, it was time to visit the Hall of Presidents. Each president was dressed in authentic period clothing, and it was hard to believe they weren't real.

"How many can you name?" Kate asked Bonnie.

"It's like my doll collection has come alive," Bonnie said about It's a Small World. There were dolls from all over the world, including yodelers from Switzerland, kite flyers from Japan, and dancers from Polynesia wearing grass skirts. Lulu liked the theme song so much she sang it over and over.

"Hold on tight," whispered Kate's dad. "We're off to Never Land." It felt like they were flying as they glided over a spectacular nighttime scene of London. Down below, thousands of tiny lights from the city twinkled, and moonlight danced on the river Thames. "Up, up, and awaaaay!"

Bonnie asked Aunt Karen if she wanted to go on the Mad Tea Party. "No thanks," laughed Aunt Karen. "It makes me too dizzy! I'll take Lulu on Dumbo instead." Lulu sat in Aunt Karen's lap and giggled and clapped as the big-eared elephant floated up and down.

At Mickey's Starland, Lulu watched a stage show starring Mickey and Minnie and her other favorite characters. She toured Mickey's house, peeked into Minnie's Dollhouse, petted baby animals at Grandma Duck's Farm, and even had her picture taken with Mickey!

After that Kate's dad said it was the perfect time for an ice-cream break.
"I want chocolate!" said Mike.
"I want vanilla!" said Rich.
"I want strawberry!" said Bonnie and Kate.

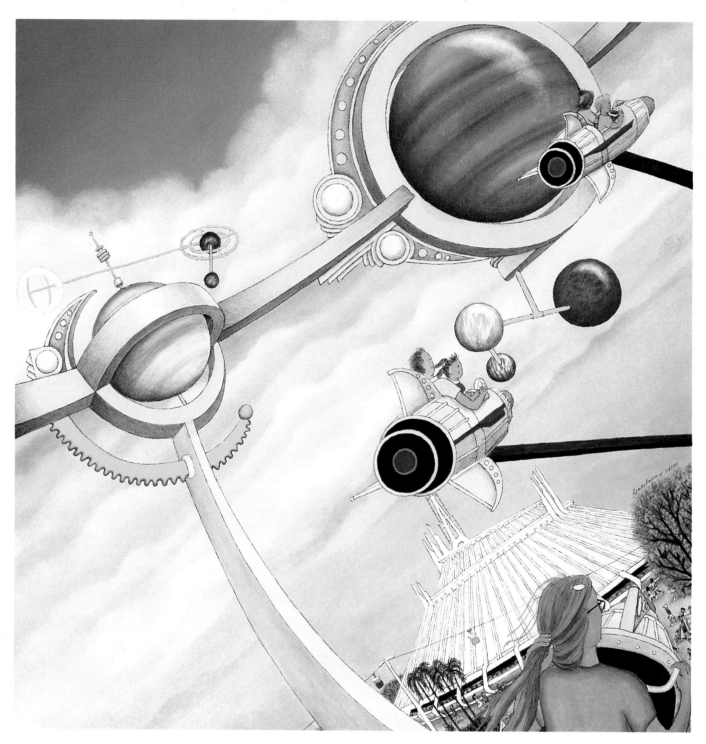

Mike and Rich said they wanted to go on Space Mountain next. "How about we ride the Astro Orbiter first?" asked Kate. From way up high they had a perfect view of the park. They could even see Aunt Karen and Lulu waving to them from way down below.

"Everyone looks like ants!" said Bonnie.

"Let's go meet a creature from outer space," said Kate as they headed toward the Extra "Terror"estrial Alien Encounter. "I bet the alien is huge and green and has three heads!"

"Sometimes I think my brother's a creature from outer space," joked Bonnie.

"It's getting late," Kate's dad said a little while later. The sun was going down, and everyone was happy but tired. Lulu had already fallen asleep by the time they stopped for dinner at a small café, and even Kate found herself yawning once or twice. It had been an exciting day. What better way to end it than by watching a spectacular SpectroMagic parade?

When the parade finally ended, it was time to go back to the hotel. Kate was so tired she could hardly keep her eyes open. She couldn't wait to go to bed. But she was also excited. After all, tomorrow was sure to be *another* magical day.

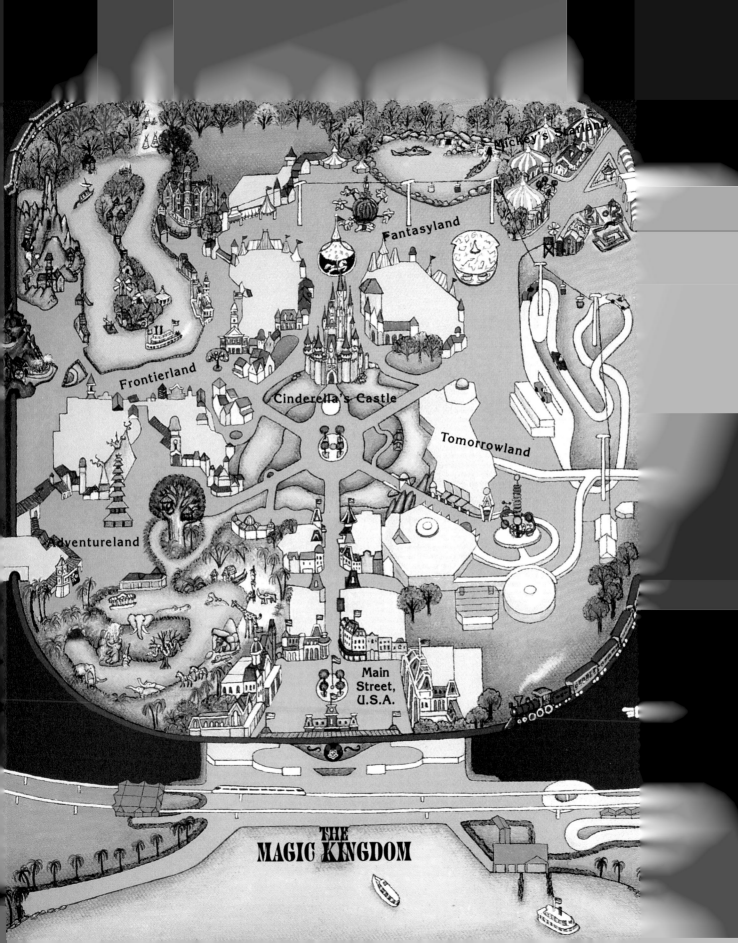

THE
MAGIC KINGDOM

Melvin the Moose
from Country Bear Jamboree.

Outside the Haunted Mansion . . .

A hitchhiking ghost!

The kitchen at Mickey's Treehouse.

The Big Thunder Mountain Railroad.

Beware of the snake on the Jungle Cruise!

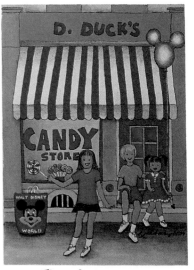

Time for a treat
at Donald Duck's Candy Store!